MILLIE BOBBY BROWN

BY JOANNE MATTERN

AMICUS LEARNING

Inspire is published by
Amicus Learning, an imprint of Amicus
P.O. Box 227
Mankato, MN 56002
www.amicuspublishing.us

Editor: Ana Brauer
Series Designer: Kathleen Petelinsek
Book Designer and Photo Researcher: Emily Dietz

Library of Congress Cataloging-in-Publication Data
Names: Mattern, Joanne, 1963- author
Title: Millie Bobby Brown / by Joanne Mattern.
Description: Mankato, MN : Amicus Learning, an imprint of Amicus, 2026. | Series: Inspire | Includes bibliographical references and index. | Audience: Ages 5–9 | Audience: Grades 2–3 | Summary: "Lights, camera, action! Discover how Millie Bobby Brown rose to fame as a child actor, from her breakthrough role as Eleven in Netflix's *Stranger Things* to starring in *Enola Holmes*. Includes table of contents, glossary, further resources, and index"— Provided by publisher.
Identifiers: LCCN 2025011926 (print) | LCCN 2025011927 (ebook) | ISBN 9798892008631 library binding | ISBN 9798892009294 paperback | ISBN 9798892009959 ebook
Subjects: LCSH: Brown, Millie Bobby, 2004—Juvenile literature | Motion picture actors and actresses—United States—Biography—Juvenile literature | Television actors and actresses—United States—Biography—Juvenile literature | LCGFT: Biographies
Classification: LCC PN2287.B697 M38 2025 (print) | LCC PN2287.B697 (ebook) | DDC 791.4302/8092 [B]—dc23/eng/20250527
LC record available at https://lccn.loc.gov/2025011926
LC ebook record available at https://lccn.loc.gov/2025011927

Photo Credits: Alamy Stock Photo/AFF, 20, Album, 16, Collection Christophel, 13, Photo12/Netflix, 14, ZUMA Press, 21; Associated Press/Anthony Behar, cover; Getty Images/Dimitrios Kambouris, 17, Frederick M. Brown, 9, Gina Pricope, 6, Isa Foltin, 19, Kevin Mazur, 5, Kevork Djansezian/BAFTA LA, 10, Steve Granitz, 15

Printed in the United States of America

Table of Contents

4 Young and Famous
7 Moving Around
8 Hard to Hear
11 What a Talent!
12 Taking a Chance
14 Stranger Things
17 Making Movies
18 Beauty Queen
21 Brown Gets Married
22 Super Stats
23 Glossary
24 Read More
24 On the Web
24 Index

Young and Famous

Millie Bobby Brown is a British actress. She has worked on many things. Brown is best known for playing Eleven in the TV series *Stranger Things*. Brown may be young. But she is very talented!

Brown started as a child actor and grew up to be a popular young star.

Orlando, Florida, was home to Brown's family when she was growing up.

Moving Around

Brown was born in Spain on February 19, 2004. When she was four years old, Brown and her family moved to England. When she was eight, the family moved to Florida.

WHAT'S IN A NAME?
Brown was given the middle name Bonnie. She started using Bobby to match her dad's name.

Hard to Hear

When Brown was born, she could not hear well with her left ear. A few years later, she became **deaf** in that ear. Even though she had trouble hearing herself, she kept on singing and acting.

Brown started acting at eight years old.

Brown's dad is one of her biggest supporters.

What a Talent!

Brown loved to act. When she was eight years old, she went to an acting camp in Orlando, Florida. A **talent scout** saw her. The scout told Brown's parents she had "**instincts** you cannot teach."

Taking a Chance

Brown and her family decided to move to Los Angeles, California. Brown soon got small parts in TV shows. But she never got any big parts. Brown's family struggled in Los Angeles. They moved back to England and lived with Brown's aunt.

In 2014, Brown had a small role in the TV show *Intruders.*

Stranger Things

Brown thought her acting career was over. Then, everything changed. In 2016, she was cast as Eleven in the Netflix show *Stranger Things*. The show was a huge hit. Brown was **nominated** for awards for her acting.

A SPECIAL GIRL

Eleven has special powers. She can move things with her mind.

Brown won an MTV award for *Stranger Things* in 2017.

Brown played Enola Holmes in 2020 and came back for two more *Enola Holmes* movies.

Making Movies

In 2019, Brown made her movie **debut**. She appeared in *Godzilla: King of the Monsters*. Later, Brown appeared in the **sequel**. It was called *Godzilla vs. Kong* (2021). She also played the lead role in *Enola Holmes* (2020).

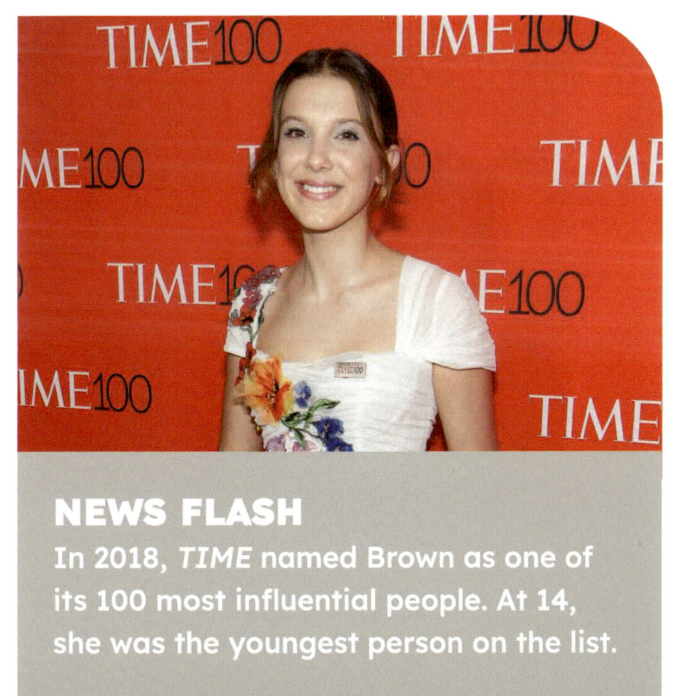

NEWS FLASH

In 2018, *TIME* named Brown as one of its 100 most influential people. At 14, she was the youngest person on the list.

Beauty Queen

In 2019, Brown started a skincare brand. It is called Florence by Mills. Brown's products help people feel beautiful, no matter what they look like. She also made sure the products were never tested on animals.

Brown named her skincare brand after her great-grandmother.

Brown poses with her husband at an event in 2025.

Brown Gets Married

In 2024, Brown married Jake Bongiovi. The couple met on Instagram in 2021. Brown was just 20 years old when she got married. The future is bright in both love and work for this talented young star!

DID YOU KNOW?
Brown's *Stranger Things* costar, Matthew Modine, **officiated** Brown's wedding.

SUPER STATS

MILLIE BOBBY BROWN

Birthday: February 19, 2004

Birthplace: Marbella, Spain

Main TV Roles: *Stranger Things* (2016-2025)

Main Movie Roles: *The Electric State* (2025), *Damsel* (2024), *Enola Holmes 2* (2022), *Godzilla vs. Kong* (2021), *Enola Holmes* (2020), *Godzilla: King of the Monsters* (2019)

AWARDS AND NOMINATIONS

Kids' Choice Awards: 2020, 2021, 2023

People's Choice Award: 2019

Teen Choice Awards: 2018, 2019

Primetime Emmy Awards Nominee: 2017, 2018

Screen Actors Guild Award: 2017

GLOSSARY

deaf Having total or partial hearing loss.

debut A person's first time performing.

instinct Acting naturally, without being taught.

nominate To choose as a candidate for election or an award.

officiate To perform a ceremony, such as a wedding.

sequel A book, movie, or television program that continues an earlier story.

talent scout A person who looks for performers.

READ MORE

Grack, Rachel. **Curious About Netflix.** Mankato, MN: Amicus Learning, 2026.

London, Martha. **Millie Bobby Brown.** Mankato, MN: Capstone Press, 2020.

ON THE WEB

Britannica: Millie Bobby Brown
https://www.britannica.com/biography/Millie-Bobby-Brown

IMDb: Millie Bobby Brown
https://www.imdb.com/name/nm5611121/bio/

INDEX

Bongiovi, Jake, 21
deafness, 8
England, 7, 12
Enola Holmes, 16, 17
Florence by Mills, 18–19
Florida, 6, 7, 11
Godzilla: King of the Monsters, 17
Los Angeles, California, 12
Modine, Matthew, 21
Stranger Things, 4, 14–15, 21
TIME, 17

About the Author

Joanne Mattern is the author of hundreds of nonfiction books for children. Her favorite subjects are biographies, sports, animals, and history. Joanne loves learning new things and sharing that knowledge with young readers! She lives in New York State with her family.